PORTCHE CASTI

HAMPSHIRE

John Goodall, PhD FSA

Portchester Castle stands imposingly on a low-lying tongue of land that projects into the natural harbour of Portsmouth. Its outer defences incorporate the magnificently preserved remains of a Roman fort, which was probably established here in the AD *280s. From the fifth century a Saxon community settled this fort, and about 904 it was turned into a stronghold or burgh, one in a chain intended to protect the kingdom of Wessex from Viking raids. Following the Norman Conquest in 1066 an important castle was established on the site, its principal buildings set in an enclosure in the north-west angle of the Roman defences. Among those that survive today are the twelfth-century great tower or keep, and a royal residence erected in the 1390s for Richard II. The castle remained occupied into the seventeenth century. It then served intermittently as a prisoner-of-war camp until the end of the Napoleonic Wars. This guidebook offers a tour of the castle and a short history of its development since the Roman period.*

CONTENTS

Published by English Heritage, 23 Savile Row, London W1S 2ET
Visit our website at www.english-heritage.org.uk
Portchester Castle, Castle Street, Portchester, Hampshire PO16 9QW
Telephone: 02392 378291
Edited by Sarah Yates. Designed by Diana Stimpson. Print production by Elaine Pooke.
Printed in England by Hawthornes.

ISBN 1 85074 766 0 02135 C55 04/05
Photographs by English Heritage Photographic Unit and copyright of English Heritage, unless otherwise stated.

TOUR OF THE CASTLE

❖

INTRODUCTION

Since they were constructed over 1,700 years ago the walls, towers and enclosing ditches of the square-planned Roman fort at Portchester have been the constant and defining element of this site. Within the huge nine-acre area they enclose great changes have taken place. As it presently exists, the interior broadly reflects the medieval arrangement of the site, when the Roman fort walls served as the defensive perimeter of a great castle. The keep and other principal castle buildings are arranged around a defended courtyard or inner bailey occupying the north-west quarter of the Roman fort. Diagonally opposite in the outer bailey, stands the parish church, all that remains of a monastic foundation established here in about 1128.

This tour begins in the inner bailey of the medieval castle and then describes the Roman fortifications of the outer bailey, and the church. There are directions throughout the tour to guide you, but should you wish to follow your own route, the aerial view on the inside front cover will help orientate you.

Go out through the door of the ticket office and turn left into the courtyard.

The walls of Portchester Castle remain the most complete of any Roman fort in Europe

INNER BAILEY

You are standing in the inner bailey, the medieval heart of Portchester Castle. Around this square-planned courtyard, dominated by the massive form of the twelfth-century keep, are the shells of several grand medieval ranges.

The inner bailey was probably laid out when the castle was first established in the late eleventh century. It sits in the north-west corner of the Roman fort and is divided from the remainder of the fort enclosure by an L-shaped ditch and wall. All the original buildings and fortifications of the inner bailey at Portchester are likely to have been of earth and timber. But in the early twelfth century these began to be replaced in stone. One of the first new stone buildings was the keep, which was probably begun around 1130. The keep and bailey buildings continued to be adapted or redeveloped throughout the Middle Ages and today are a complicated combination of different periods of construction. Their magnificent remains provide a fascinating insight into the changing face of this great castle through the medieval period and beyond.

A view of the keep with the ruined forebuilding beneath. The lines of sockets in the walls of the tower are fixings for the medieval scaffold

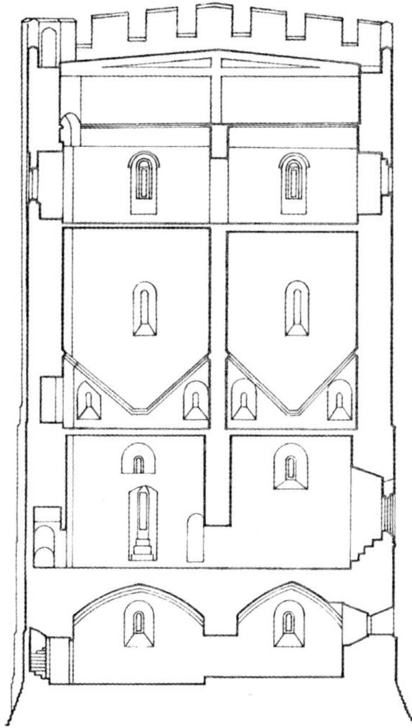

Go into the centre of the courtyard towards the fixed information panel beside the path, so as to get a good view of the keep.

KEEP

This tower has always been the architectural showpiece and symbolic focus of the castle. Built on a square plan, it stands more than 30 m (100 ft) high, and its thick walls are faced with small, beautifully cut stones. Visible in the walls are lines of regularly spaced sockets, the fixings for the medieval scaffold used in its construction. In the twelfth century the keep contained some of the most important apartments in the castle.

Despite its uniform appearance today, the keep was actually built in three stages. As it was first completed in the 1130s, it rose to a point approximately level with the tops of the buttresses around the exterior. But probably within twenty years of its completion this low structure was almost doubled in height with the addition of two upper storeys. Finally the crown of the building was raised in the 1320s. During the 1390s the basement of the tower was vaulted, and several new windows were inserted in the principal first-floor chambers.

As is typical of twelfth-century keeps, that at Portchester has its main entrance at first-floor level. This was approached up an external stair housed within a subsidiary tower or forebuilding. The forebuilding was extensively altered over the Middle Ages and is now largely ruined. The modern wooden stair – built up against the bailey wall to your right (north) – follows the line of a lost twelfth-century predecessor. At ground level immediately to the left (south) of the stair was a prison chamber and above this a chapel. The blind arch in the keep wall would originally have faced into the chapel interior and may have served as an architectural frame for the king's throne when he attended services here. Above the arch are the incised lines of different roofs, evidence of the many alterations the forebuilding has undergone.

A cross-section of the keep looking westwards. The building is divided by a central spine wall and was raised in three principal stages. Note the V-shaped outlines of the roof to the first tower within what is now the second floor of the building

A cut-away illustration of the forebuilding as it existed in the twelfth century. The chapel is on the upper floor to the left

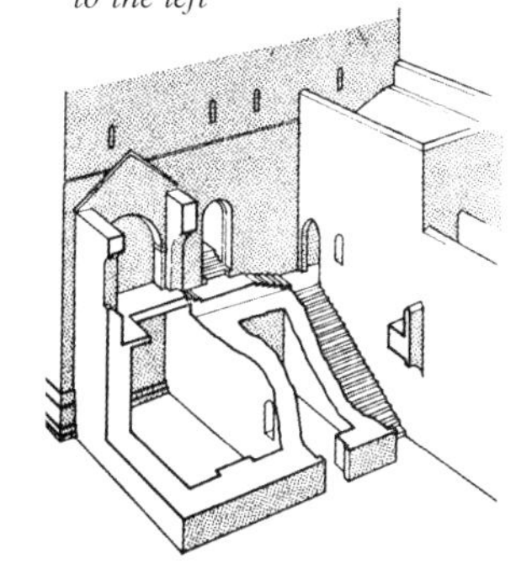

JOHN GOODALL

A detail of the damaged ornament to the first-floor keep windows. The detailing compares to that found in the priory church

To the right of the wooden stair, within a tower projecting beyond the Roman wall, was a large first-floor chamber. It possibly served as a waiting room for visitors to the keep and was provided in the later Middle Ages with a grand bay window, probably inserted about 1489: the remains of a contemporary window on the south courtyard face of the forebuilding to your left are decorated with a shield bearing the arms of Henry VII (reigned 1485–1509).

Archaeological excavation of the inner bailey has revealed that in the 1320s the forebuilding was enclosed on its courtyard faces by other buildings, and a new main stair to the keep was erected. No trace of these buildings now remains above ground, but a diagonal line of sockets, the settings for the steps of the 1320s stair, is visible in the east face of the forebuilding.

Go along the path and up the wooden stairs into the keep.

JOHN GOODALL

The first-floor entrance chamber of the keep must have been very imposing in the twelfth century. It originally had a flat ceiling, large, richly ornamented windows and a well

First floor

Our understanding of the keep as a living medieval building is complicated by the many alterations it has undergone, in particular the insertion of extra floors to lodge 3,000 prisoners during the Napoleonic Wars. It is arranged today on four levels separated by three modern timber floors and is divided through almost its full height by a central or spine wall, creating two principal chambers on each floor. Access between the floors was originally provided only by a spiral stair in the south-west angle of the building, but a modern wooden stair now also rises up the northern side of the keep from the first floor.

The first-floor chambers of the keep were probably intended to function together in the twelfth century as a domestic suite. Although now badly damaged and comfortless, the room entered directly from the forebuilding stair would have been well suited for the reception of important visitors. To the left of the entrance, in the south-east corner of the chamber, is a well and in the adjacent south wall two large and richly ornamented windows, one of which is now blocked. There is also a latrine in the thickness of the outer keep wall at the far end of the room, though access to this is now obstructed by concrete beams inserted to stabilise the keep in the 1930s. The room originally had a

Divided from the entrance chamber by the spine wall is this large room. It contains the only fireplace in the building (right) and has small windows. It may originally have served as a royal bedchamber

flat, panelled wooden ceiling, some fixings for which still remain. Richly painted and furnished this could have been a splendid interior in the twelfth century.

The second chamber is entered through the doorway at the far (west) end of the central partition wall. This must have served as an inner apartment, possibly a bedroom or withdrawing chamber. Although entirely devoid of architectural ornament, it is the only room in the keep with a fireplace, now a ragged opening in the centre of the outside wall to your left. This lacked a proper chimney, the smoke escaping through openings in the wall. In the north-east corner of the chamber is a small latrine. The door of this has been ripped away, but a little wall niche for a candle is still visible.

Climb up the modern timber stair to the second floor of the keep.

Second floor

Before the keep was first heightened in the mid-twelfth century it would appear that the roof of the building was set within this second-floor level: projecting from the end walls of both chambers is a narrow ledge of stone that clearly follows the V-shaped outline of a double-pitched roof. In its original form, therefore, this floor must have comprised a series of loft spaces, lit at either end by small windows. Directly accessible from the main spiral stair, these lofts may have been used for storage, or to lodge members of the household or servants. One anomalous feature of this arrangement is that the four divisions of the roof would presumably have created four separate loft spaces,

Preserved within the massively tall second-floor level are the V-shaped roof valleys of the original keep. This roof was removed when the keep was heightened

JOHN GOODALL

each inaccessible to the other. Yet if this was so, how was the door in the central spine wall accessed?

With the raising of the keep about 1150 this roof level became a floor. But the fact that the redundant lines of the original keep roof are preserved here indicates that no attempt was made to finish off the interiors of this new floor as comfortable apartments. Rather, it seems as if the keep was heightened simply to turn it into a vastly taller building. To this end the second floor was elevated to a height of nearly 10 m (30 ft) and a top storey added. This upper level was provided with a latrine chamber and was clearly intended for domestic use. But, as its plain architectural detailing suggests, the comforts of the top storey can never have approached those of the first-floor apartments, and it possible served as a guardchamber.

A reconstruction of the interior of the keep when it was racked out for the accommodation of prisoners in the Napoleonic Wars. Conditions within the building must have been appalling

The massive internal spaces of the upper section of the keep have been variously partitioned since the Middle Ages. Judging from the socket marks that cover the walls numerous timbers have been removed from within it. Some of these relate to lost floors inserted between the medieval levels, but others served as racking on which to sling prisoners' hammocks during the Napoleonic Wars.

Go through into the second chamber of the second floor and up the metal stair to the mezzanine balcony to view the remains of the theatre wall paintings. Descend from the balcony and go back into the first chamber, and then up to the top of the wooden stair.

Third floor and roof

When the keep was first heightened in about 1150, the roof was replaced at the level where the central partition wall terminates. Another floor was added, perhaps around 1320, and the roof raised to its present position. The inserted floor has now been removed and the roof is modern.

Go up the spiral stair in the far chamber of the third floor onto the roof.

THE CASTLE THEATRE

Faintly visible on the walls around you are the remains of an elaborate painted decorative scheme for the auditorium of an early nineteenth-century theatre within the keep. The scheme attempts to create the illusion of an interior hung with rich objects: along the side walls is a series of panels within elaborate frames and between them small landscape scenes, one of which depicts Portchester Castle. Around the tops of the walls are painted swags of fabric.

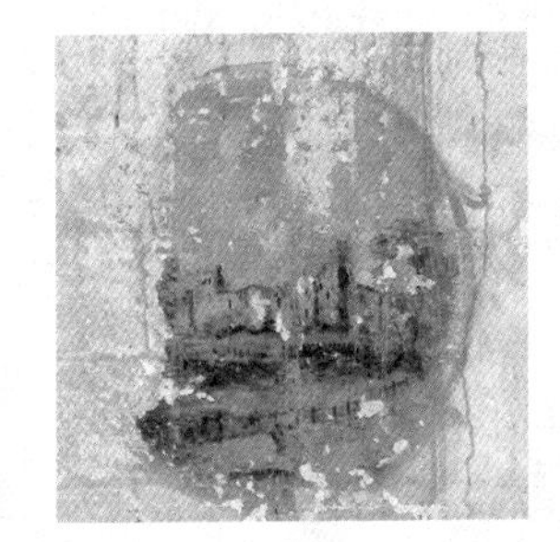

The roundel painting of the castle

Very little is known about the history of this theatre. The style of painting suggests an early nineteenth-century Continental origin for the scheme and it might, therefore, be supposed to have been created by French prisoners of war. But one pigment used in the scheme – French Ultramarine – only came into use after 1830, after the prison had closed. In fact the theatre must have been created by a certain Mr Sutton, who is credited by J. H. Cooke, in a local history book published in 1930, with having produced plays in the keep. Unfortunately, it is not clear whether Sutton was an actor or manager of the theatre.

STEPHEN CONLIN

A reconstruction drawing of the theatre showing its design in relation to the present viewing platform. The roof and floor levels of this room are modern

A view of the castle and harbour from the keep roof. The church within the Roman walls is an exceptional survival, the remains of an Augustinian priory that existed here briefly in the twelfth century

From the top of the keep there is a magnificent view over the castle and its surroundings. The commanding position of the castle within Portsmouth harbour is easy to appreciate. Visible in the surrounding landscape are many forts and batteries built since the sixteenth century to defend this important harbour.

Return down the spiral stair to the third floor and retrace your route down the wooden stair, back into the inner bailey courtyard.

Richard II's palace

Extending from the foot of the keep around the west and south sides of the inner bailey are the remains of a grand series of residential apartments built by Richard II (reigned 1377–99) as part of his reorganisation of the castle between 1396 and 1399. There are two principal ranges, both two storeys high. That in front of you – to the south – is the public and service wing, which contains the great hall and kitchens. To your right – to the west – are the inner royal apartments, including the king's great chamber.

The principal chambers in each range are on the first floor, an arrangement indicated on the exterior by the tall windows round this level of the buildings. These upper chambers were connected by a vaulted passage at the angle of the courtyard, and a medieval visitor would have moved through them in

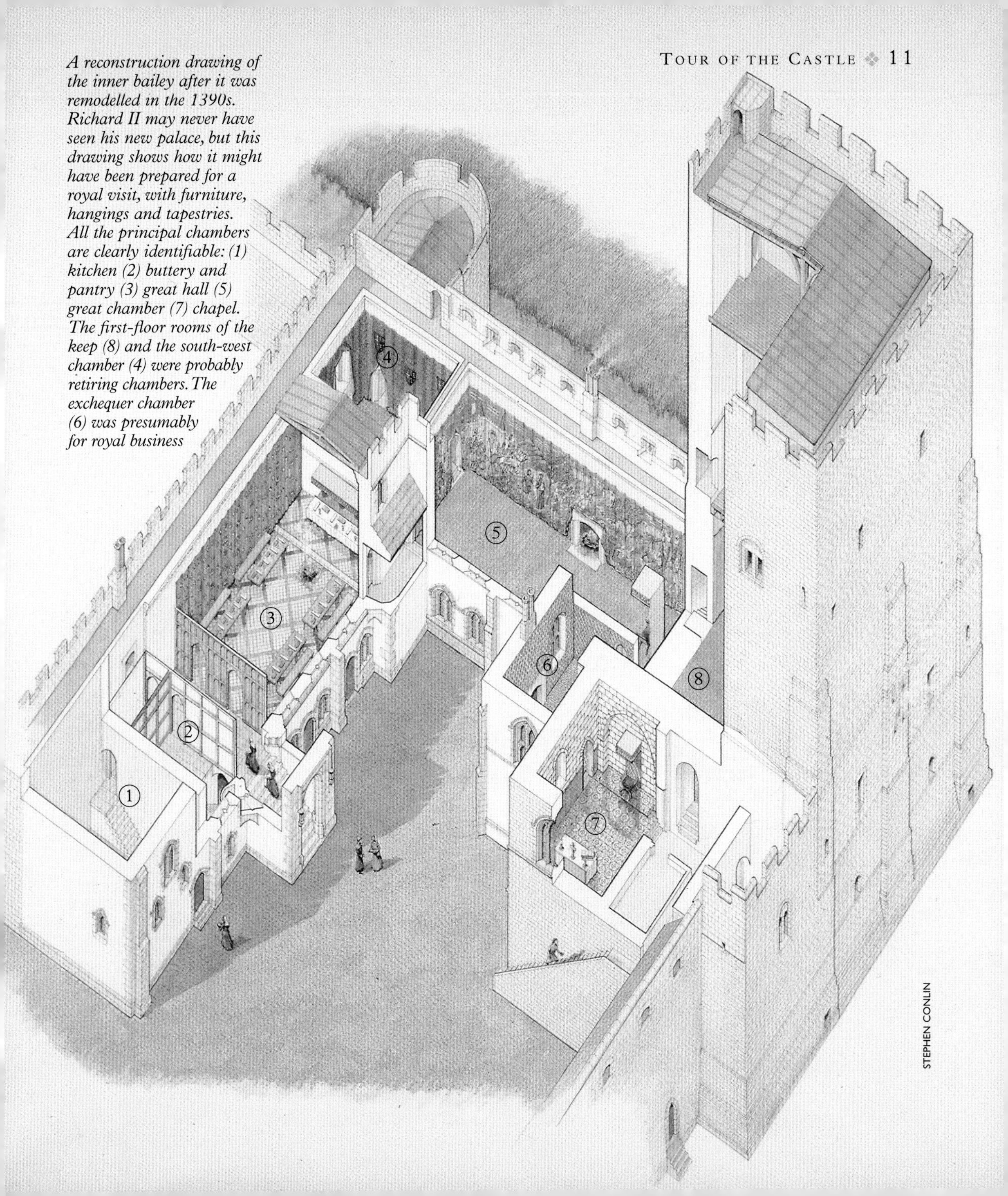

A reconstruction drawing of the inner bailey after it was remodelled in the 1390s. Richard II may never have seen his new palace, but this drawing shows how it might have been prepared for a royal visit, with furniture, hangings and tapestries. All the principal chambers are clearly identifiable: (1) kitchen (2) buttery and pantry (3) great hall (5) great chamber (7) chapel. The first-floor rooms of the keep (8) and the south-west chamber (4) were probably retiring chambers. The exchequer chamber (6) was presumably for royal business

a particular sequence, from the public great hall to the king's innermost chamber. Such planning is typical of palace interiors of this period.

Beneath this suite of royal apartments were several rooms, each accessible through a separate door from the courtyard. These have smaller windows than the rooms on the floor above and were probably used for storage and accommodation.

Porch

Entrance to the royal apartments on the first floor was through the projecting porch in the middle of the great hall range. To either side of its entrance are two curious pedestals with hat-shaped covers set above them. These are housings for lamps to light the threshold. Rising up from this entrance door was a stair, now lost, to the first-floor door of the hall. This stair was covered by a miniature stone vault – of which the stubs remain. Above the vault was a tiny chamber, reached by a spiral stair from the porch landing.

Go through the door immediately to the left of the porch of the great hall range.

JOHN GOODALL

A view of the great hall range. To the left of the porch are the service rooms – the kitchen, buttery and pantry. Beyond the porch is the great hall and to the far right the great chamber range

Kitchen

The great hall range is now a roofless shell, incorporating the twelfth-century inner bailey wall along its south side. It is divided into two unequal areas by a stone wall: you are in the smaller of these, the kitchen. Partitioning this from the rest of the range was probably intended as a safeguard against the spread of fire. The kitchen is very small by medieval standards and was presumably served by a centrally placed fire. A building account records that in 1398 a louver was erected to release the smoke from this. Food would have been carried into the great hall via a stair (now ruined) through the raised door in one corner of the kitchen.

The door of the great hall porch, with brackets for lamps to light the threshold

Pass through the door to your right into the main part of the great hall range.

Great hall

To the west of the kitchen wall the range was divided into an upper and lower level by a wooden floor, the position of which is indicated by the threshold to the door at the head of the porch stairs to your right. Stone walls separated the ground-floor chambers, and the lines of these are still visible. But on the floor above all the partitions were of wood, and the complex arrangement of the interior must be inferred from the position of doors and windows.

In the small area between the kitchen wall and the porch door an intermediate floor was inserted to create three rectangular chambers on ground-, first- and second-floor levels. The uppermost chamber, which also had access to the room over the porch, may have been the lodging of a senior household servant. But the two chambers beneath are likely to have been service chambers – probably a buttery and pantry – and were internally connected by a flight of steps, the base for which survives.

The east end of the great hall has a complex grouping of doors and windows. They indicate the existence of lost floor and partitions

The remainder of the upper floor was occupied by the great hall. This must have been a splendid chamber, open to the roof and lit down one side by high windows. According to the building accounts, the glass in the windows of this and the other principal chambers was decorated with coats of arms and heraldic borders. The hall was heated by a fire set centrally on an open hearth, the square foundation for which remains at ground level. Along the top of the windowless south wall are fragments of a carved stone frieze that originally ran round the interior. Like the wall frieze of the great hall at Westminster, London, perhaps Richard II's most celebrated building, it appears to depict beasts and heraldic devices. The blank wall may also have been decorated with wall paintings and been intended – during royal visits only – for the display of tapestries, of which Richard II had a large collection.

A medieval visitor would not have entered directly into the hall from the porch. As was typical in English great halls, the main entrance as well as the kitchen and service doors were concealed from the body of the room by a screen. The area enclosed by this partition – which effectively formed a corridor across the building from north to south – was known as the screen's passage. It was located at what was termed the 'low' end of the hall, the area commonly accessible to the whole household and its servants.

NATIONAL MONUMENTS RECORD

Richard II's most celebrated architectural project was the remodelling of Westminster Hall, London, from 1393. The hall at Portchester had an internal cornice carved with beasts, similar to that seen here. At Westminster all the beasts are turned to face the king's throne

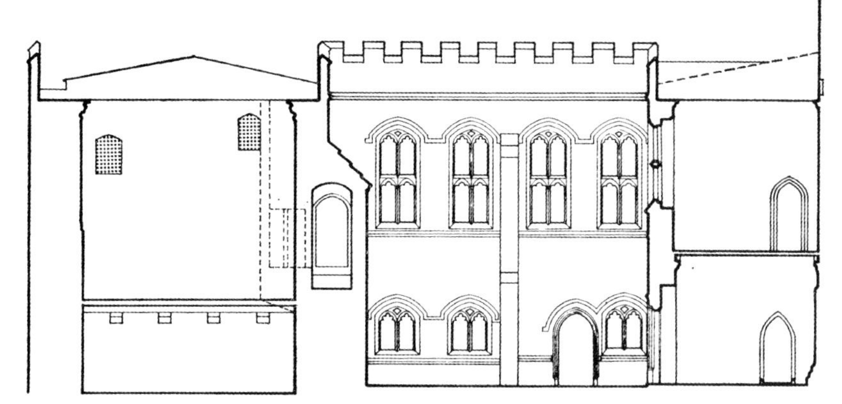

A reconstruction of the great chamber range. The systematic use of single- and double-tier windows to light the two floors is a distinctive feature of other fourteenth-century buildings in castles such as Windsor and Bodiam

At the opposite end was the 'high' end of the hall, where the king's table stood, raised on a dais. The building accounts suggest that a timber canopy was set up over the table to indicate its importance. Other tables would have lined the sides of the room between the dais and the screen's passage, and members of the household would have sat at these in strict hierarchical order.

To be allowed to pass beyond the great hall into the chamber range was a mark of distinction. To do so, a visitor would have had to walk up onto the dais and through the door in the north wall to the right. From here a vaulted passage leads to the upper floor of the adjacent range, where the king's inner apartments were located. Immediately below the dais doorway in the north wall of the great hall range are the fragmentary remains of two richly carved arches. From their detailing these would appear to date from the early twelfth century and show that Richard II's ranges incorporate the remains of much earlier buildings. It is not known what these looked like or what function the chambers within them served, but to judge from these arches they were grand structures.

Within the north wall of the great hall are these fragments of richly carved arches, surviving remains of grand twelfth-century buildings on this site

The curious windows of the chamber in the south-west angle of the inner bailey. The doors to the right led to a Roman bastion fitted with latrines, now demolished

Go out into the courtyard and through the door in the adjacent west range to your left.

Great chamber range

The passage from the dais of the great hall led into the larger of two rooms that occupied the upper floor of the west or great chamber range. This was probably the king's great chamber or formal reception room and was heated by a large, central fireplace, now a ragged hole in the wall. To the south of the great chamber, and divided from it by a stone wall, was a small room, identified by some scholars as the royal bedchamber. Both this room and that immediately below it have windows arranged like fireplaces,with narrow flues letting in light from small holes (now blocked) in the wall above. Presumably this was a defensive measure, reflecting the builders' reluctance to insert large windows in the inner bailey wall. Running beneath the great chamber were two rooms, each with a brick-backed fireplace. Like all the interiors in this range, the ceilings of these rooms were edged with cornices projecting from the face of the wall.

The outline of the lost, low-pitched roof to the great chamber range is still etched on the keep wall. Beneath this, the line of another single-pitch roof from an earlier range is also visible. Opening off the great chamber range beneath the keep are two further rooms built by Richard II. Their original function is not known, but the upper room may have been the 'exchequer chamber', a room for financial and legal work, described in the 1390s building accounts. A door from this chamber

The interior of the two-storey west or great chamber range with its damaged fireplaces. Lines of several roofs are cut into the keep, evidence of many generations of buildings

connects with the forebuilding chapel and, through this, with the keep beyond.

Go back into the courtyard and across the lawn to face the east range, with Ashton's Tower to your left.

East ranges

Of the three ranges that enclosed the east end of the inner bailey little now remains. To your left (north) are the foundations of a twelfth-century building that served in the late Middle Ages as the residence of the constable of the castle. It comprised a hall and vaulted undercroft and was remodelled several times. Ashton's Tower, at the east end of the residence, was begun by a constable of that name who served here between 1376 and 1381. A building account records that the tower was completed in 1385, also that work to the 'knight's chamber' – possibly the chamber over the Roman bastion behind the constable's hall – was then underway. The chambers within Ashton's Tower served as an extension to the constable's residence and are provided with large windows, fireplaces and latrines. Within the tower at wall-walk level is an internal firing gallery, the arrangement of which is best viewed from outside the castle (see pp. 19-20).

Extending across the bailey to the right (south) of Ashton's Tower is a ruined stone range. In the thirteenth century this was only one storey high, and housed a storeroom or stable to the north and a kitchen to the south. By the end of the fourteenth century the range had been largely rebuilt, one end of it being absorbed into the constable's residence. This structure was completely remodelled in the early seventeenth century by the last constable of the castle, Sir Thomas

Ashton's Tower from the inner bailey. The constable's hall originally extended to the left of this building. The medieval east range (right) was heightened in the seventeenth century

Bottom left: A detail of the ornamented window on the south face of Ashton's Tower

Below: Detail of St Michael from a painting in the Tower of London, a rare survival of secular painted decoration from Richard II's reign

TERRY BALL

A cut-away of the firing gallery around Ashton's Tower. This is one of the earliest surviving examples of purpose built artillery fortification in Britain

Cornwallis. He built the upper floor of the range as an extra series of lodgings and inserted the window frames and fireplaces you see today. These alterations were part of a wider project to remodel the whole of the constable's house, including the lost hall block to the north.

The south range now houses the ticket office and shop. It was also remodelled by Cornwallis as a kitchen, and its walls incorporate many re-used fragments of Romanesque sculpture.

Having explored the eastern ranges of the inner bailey, go back through the ticket office and out through the gatehouse. Cross the drawbridge and continue to your left along the bank of the moat until you reach the information panel fixed in the grass at the corner of the inner bailey.

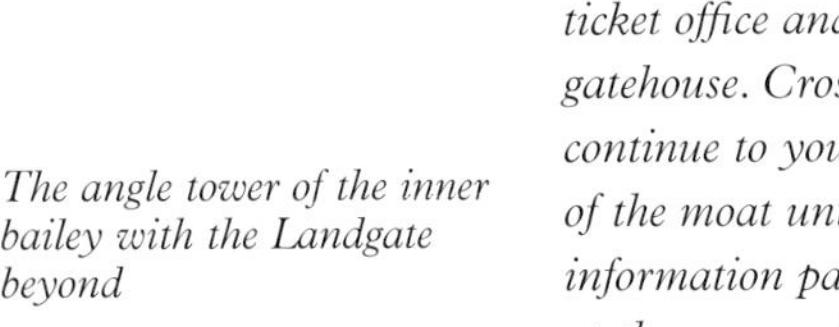

The angle tower of the inner bailey with the Landgate beyond

INNER BAILEY MOAT AND GATEHOUSE

The wall that encloses the inner bailey is faced with small blocks of cut stone, an early twelfth-century style of masonry similar to that of the keep. A castellated parapet would originally have run along the top of the wall. At the angle of the moat is a fine projecting twelfth-century tower on a square plan with an open back.

In the Middle Ages the moat around the bailey was probably deeper and wider than at present. Its inner bank may also have been raised to conceal a clearly defined band of rubble masonry along the foot of the wall. This detail is clearest in the east wall of the bailey to your right. The moat originally extended round the entire circuit of the inner bailey, both within and outside the Roman fort enclosure. Fed from the sea, a culvert below ground level allowed water to pass between its inner and outer sections. The medieval moat had largely silted up by the eighteenth century, when the eastern stretch was re-cut as a swimming pool for prisoners. It was re-created in its present form in the 1930s.

An open-backed tower projecting from the bailey wall formed the original gatehouse between the medieval inner bailey and the surrounding Roman fort enclosure. This tower still survives but its fortifications were subsequently extended forward in stages. Immediately in front of it stands a vaulted porch of the 1320s closed by a portcullis. This is flanked on either side by the ruined remains of small, thirteenth-century D-shaped towers. Built beyond these is a long, walled passage with a drawbridge pit beneath, probably of the 1380s. At the end of this passage are two square towers, built about 1600 to operate a second drawbridge over the moat.

The gatehouse to the inner bailey has gradually been extended forward and preserves a remarkable succession of drawbridge pits

Continue around the moat to the north postern gate in the Roman wall. Visitors with limited mobility may find it easier to return to the Landgate and follow the Outer bailey tour from there.

OUTER BAILEY
NORTH POSTERN GATE

This postern or side gate stands in the position of a Roman predecessor, also a small arched opening in the wall. It was one of the four original entrances into the fort enclosure and was situated opposite another secondary Roman gate in the south wall of the fort, now lost. The inner face of the Roman wall, to the left of the gate, has been roughly hacked away – the result of medieval quarrying to provide building stone for the castle. Only around the inner bailey is the Roman wall of its original thickness.

Pass through the postern gate and proceed left towards the keep along the inner bank of the moat. Stop when you come level to the square outline of Ashton's Tower at the north-east corner of the inner bailey.

NORTH WALL

From here it is possible to appreciate the manner in which the Roman wall, with its D-shaped bastions or towers, has been incorporated into the medieval defences. This stretch of wall is of particular interest because it features a mid-fourteenth-century

The medieval north postern gate stands in place of a Roman predecessor

A view of Ashton's Tower from the north east. The door at wall-walk level connects the firing gallery of the inner bailey to the outer bailey defences

A surviving latrine outlet, which spans the angle of the inner bailey wall and a Roman bastion

A view of the keep and forebuilding from the north east. Both structures project beyond the line of the Roman defences

cannon fortification, one of the earliest-known examples in English architecture. Running along the wall head is a covered passage with gun loops, many now badly damaged. This gallery runs unbroken around the inside of Ashton's Tower. From the tower a door in the gallery opens onto the Roman wall walk of the outer fort enclosure. Beyond Ashton's Tower is one of the Roman D-shaped towers. Bridging the angle between it and the wall is a large arch, an outlet for a series of medieval latrines.

Go along the outside of the wall until you reach the foot of the keep.

The keep stands across the north-west angle of the Roman fort, which must have been demolished to accommodate it. Projecting from the wall beneath it is the forebuilding with the remains of an elaborate fifteenth-century bay window. These two external facades of the keep are much plainer than those facing onto the inner bailey: their only ornament is a band of billet carving at first-floor level and a few small windows. Rising from the massive stepped base plinth are regularly spaced buttresses: at the feet of two are outlet chutes for the latrines in the chambers above.

Visible on the exterior of the keep is one architectural curiosity: the ground-floor windows are double-splayed, that is to say that the aperture is narrowest in the middle of the wall, not on its inner or outer face. This rare arrangement has been cited as evidence that the keep encases an earlier building, the original external faces of which corresponded to the position of the windows at their narrowest. The date and precise form of such a structure – if it ever existed – remain a matter for speculation.

The remains of the oriel window probably inserted into the forebuilding about 1489

Beyond the car park to your right is the line of an outer medieval ditch running across the neck of the peninsula on which the castle stands. It was probably dug in the 1320s as an extra line of defence.

Continue left around the corner of the keep and along the line of the wall until you arrive at the square stone platform projecting into the lawn.

WEST WALL

The Roman fort was laid out symmetrically. Around its square perimeter were twenty regularly positioned D-shaped towers, of which, remarkably, sixteen remain. This low table of stone is the foundation of one of the four lost towers; it was adapted to house latrines in the Middle Ages and demolished after 1790. It is of interest because it shows how the foundations of the Roman fortifications were laid. The base of a trench about 1.5 m (5 ft) deep was filled with a rammed mixture of flint and chalk and sealed with a layer of mortar. Laid into the mortar was a raft of squared timbers framed together. It is the impression of these, long rotted away, that forms the channels in this foundation.

Above this the D-shaped upper section of the tower, originally hollow and open-backed, was erected. Each tower was provided with a drain to allow rainwater to escape from the interior. There is no evidence that any of the towers at Portchester projected above the level of the wall walk or had any internal floors in the manner of some late Roman Continental examples. The raised doors in the wall here belong to the medieval reworking of this structure as a latrine tower.

Continue alongside the west wall to the main gate into the fort.

A view of the keep from the south west. The projecting foundation of the demolished Roman bastion is visible to the bottom right

ROMAN BUILDING ❖ METHODS ❖

Between the two D-shaped towers beyond (south) of the Landgate it is possible to get a good impression of the Roman defences. The walls still stand to what is probably their original height of 6.1 m (20 ft), although their upper levels and parapets are medieval. They were constructed in sections, and some of the vertical divisions between these are visible. The sections were raised in horizontal layers: a complete course of flints was set in position across the head of the wall and then covered with mortar, which bonded the stones together. Large flints were used on the faces of the wall, and courses of large limestone or brick slabs were used in some places to strengthen the masonry. Extensive refacing, both medieval and modern, has obscured these details in many areas. Wooden poles were also laid right through the original 3.1 m (10 ft) width of the wall to stabilise the structure while the mortar set. Some of the sockets for fixing the Roman scaffold are still visible in the masonry. The constructional details of the walls are best viewed from the interior of the fort.

Reconstruction drawing of Roman builders at work constructing the defences. The walls are being erected layer by layer in sections

LANDGATE

Set mid-way along each wall of the Roman fort was a gate: two principal ones to the east and west, and two secondary postern gates to the north (see p. 19) and south. The building before you is a medieval reworking of the northern entrance known as the Landgate. In its present form the gate dates largely from the 1390s and takes the form of a square tower with a vaulted gate passage and an upper lodging chamber. This chamber was later used as a detention cell for refractory prisoners. Incorporated within the inner end of the gate passage is a twelfth-century arch, the remains of an earlier Romanesque gate. Building accounts record that

The Landgate stands within the forecourt of the original Roman fort entrance

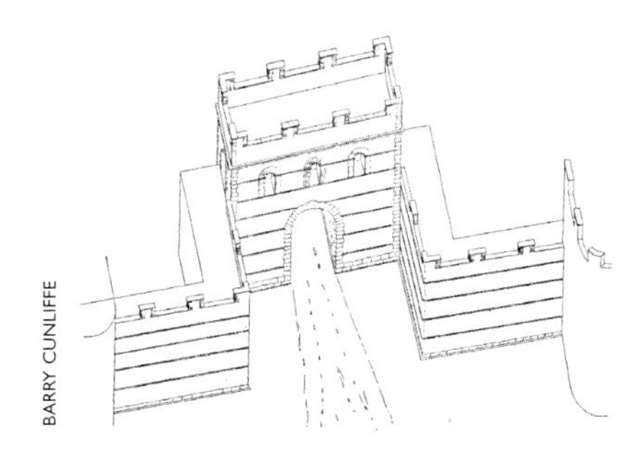
BARRY CUNLIFFE

A reconstruction of the Landgate as it might have appeared in Roman times

in 1336–7 an additional fortification was built in front of the gate, which perhaps related to the curious blocked openings in the main façade.

This building replaces an unusual Roman entrance arrangement comparable to that found in the Roman fort of Pevensey (in Sussex) down the coast. The Roman gatehouse was also rectangular in plan, with a central gate passage set between two ground-floor guard chambers. But it stood well behind the line of the wall, which turned inwards to meet it. Traces of a timber building erected within the Roman gate forecourt in the Anglo-Saxon period have been discovered.

Instead of entering the fort, continue along the west wall.

Running in front of the wall are the remains of a ditch. This feature was recut in the 1930s and follows the line of a Roman double ditch that probably enclosed the entire fort perimeter.

Continue anticlockwise around the fort until you reach the Watergate on the east side of the defences. Note the outlets for the monastic latrines in the wall as you approach the south-east corner of the fort on the seashore.

WATERGATE

The Watergate is a two-storey tower on a rectangular plan, originally with a lodging chamber on the upper floor. It stands on the main east–west axis of the fort and replaces a Roman entrance arrangement identical to that found at the Landgate. With the exception of its innermost arch (see p. 24) the present structure was largely built between 1321 and 1325. But the gate was subsequently damaged by the encroaching sea, as was the Roman wall along this side of the fort. Repairs to the gatehouse in 1369 probably included the

A line of outlets for the monastic latrines survives at the south-east corner of the fort enclosure

The interior face of the Watergate with its early inner arch

The richly ornamented west front of the priory church. Its sculpted detail compares in some points to that in the keep

construction of its front section, which projects beyond the line of the Roman wall. This addition was closed by a portcullis, the chase for which survives. The gatehouse underwent further repair in 1397–8.

Pass through the Watergate into the fort enclosure.

INTERIOR OF THE FORT

Very little is known about the interior of the fort in the Roman period. The interior may never actually have been completed in the third century, and any remains have been largely destroyed by ploughing and later occupation. Most of the buildings in it were probably of wood and regularly laid out around the roads connecting the four entrances to the fort. The principal of these ran roughly along the line of the modern road between the Landgate and Watergate. It was lightly metalled and had a central drain.

Several Saxon buildings have been excavated on the site, but today nothing is visible of this period of occupation, with the possible exception of the arch of the Watergate behind you. This arch, with different coloured stones laid alternately, has been compared to that in the Anglo-Saxon church porch at nearby Titchfield and dated to the tenth century. But it may equally be an early Norman structure of the following century.

To your left stands the parish church of St Mary [not in the care of English Heritage], all that remains of a short-lived Augustinian monastery within the fort. This was founded about 1128 but by 1150 had moved to a site at nearby Southwick, possibly because the castle lacked enough space. Judging from its architectural decoration, the church was probably under construction in the 1130s, though it is not known whether the structure or the monastic buildings were ever completed before the community moved.

A view of the inner bailey and keep from the south east

HISTORY OF THE CASTLE

Roman Portchester

Many different opinions have been offered about the date at which the Roman fort at Portchester was first established. But coin finds from the recent excavations suggest that it was built by a certain Marcus Aurelius Carausius between AD 285 and 290. If this is correct, it allows us to determine in some detail the circumstances in which the fort was constructed.

Carausius rose to prominence during the reign of Emperor Diocletian and in 285 was commissioned to clear the North Sea of barbarian pirates. He was successful in his campaigns but was accused – with what truth it is now impossible to tell – of enriching himself unscrupulously on the spoils of the pirates, only attacking their ships when they were laden with plunder. Either for this reason or because of political jealousy, a plot was hatched to have Carausius executed. But he heard of it and in response proclaimed himself

ARCHAEOLOGY AT PORTCHESTER

Our knowledge of the history of Portchester has been transformed in recent years by an extensive programme of archaeological excavation under the direction of Professor Barry Cunliffe. Between 1961 and 1979 about one third of the fort interior was excavated. The work has shed light on every phase of the history of the site, from its undocumented development in the Roman and Saxon periods to its use as a prisoner-of-war camp in the nineteenth century. Numerous specialists have contributed to the analysis of the excavations, and their findings have been published in five substantial volumes by the Society of Antiquaries of London.

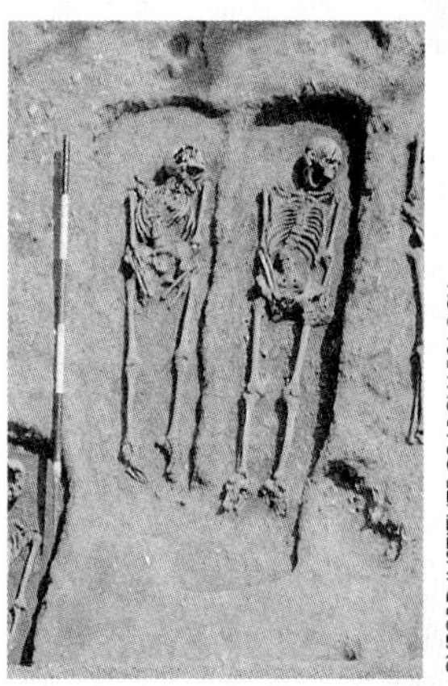

OXFORD INSTITUTE OF ARCHAEOLOGY

A photograph taken during excavation of the Saxon cemetry

The imposing southern face of the fort gives some impression of the scale of the Roman defences. A double ditch also probably enclosed the site

an emperor. Initially he controlled parts of Gaul (France) and Britain, but in 293 the last of his Continental possessions – Boulogne – was lost to the forces of Rome. Later that year he was assassinated by a follower called Alectus, who in turn proclaimed himself ruler of Britain. But in 296 a full-scale invasion of Britain finally brought the province back under central Roman authority.

The early development of Portchester Castle can be tied in very neatly with these events. Barbarian attacks along the coasts of Gaul and Britain were evidently a problem for the Roman empire throughout the late third century, and to combat them numerous forts were constructed or remodelled on both sides of the Channel. These have many features in common, in particular projecting D-shaped towers, a novel feature of Roman military architecture at this date. The forts probably acted as naval bases from which ships could intercept attacks by pirates as they were funnelled together by the narrowing of the Channel towards the Straits of Dover. Commanding this natural bottleneck were the Roman fleets in Boulogne and Dover.

A coin minted by Carausius, self-proclaimed emperor and the builder of Portchester Castle

BRITISH MUSEUM

While barbarian pirates were contained by these defences the south coast of Britain was safe. But

Carausius's appointment coincided with a particularly intensive period of attacks, which might explain why Portchester was built. If the pirates had begun regularly to penetrate the Straits of Dover, bases for military operations would have been needed all along this ill-defended stretch of the coast. For this purpose Portchester could have been supported or superseded by the Roman fort at Pevensey, also set above a natural harbour about 80 km (50 miles) to the east. This fort has recently been shown to be a work of the 290s and shares some striking architectural similarities with Portchester.

Two circumstances revealed by the recent archaeological investigations are further consistent with the fort being constructed between 285 and 290. First, there is a gap in finds of coins from the 290s, which suggests that the fort was deserted for a short period soon after it was completed. Second, there is little trace of buildings in the earliest phase of occupation, and such ditches and road surfaces as have been discovered look makeshift. It appears, therefore, as if the fort was constructed to deal with an immediate crisis but was then abandoned before being completed, most probably because Carausius's victories had rendered it redundant.

But Portchester did not remain vacant long: there is evidence that it was occupied once more from about AD 300, though how the site was developed is not clear. Around the mid-fourth century the interior of the fort was reordered with new roads. This work may have been undertaken as part of the improvement of the defences of Britain ordered by Emperor Constans, who visited the province in 342.

SKYSCAN BALLOON PHOTOGRAPHY

Built in the 290s AD the walls and towers of Pevensey Castle compare closely to those of Portchester. This fort was also the site of a later castle

PETER DUNN

A reconstruction drawing of Roman Portchester from the south-east c. 350 AD. The towers of the fort were probably level with the wall walks, not raised above them

❖ THE *NOTITIA DIGNITATUM* ❖

Of the community living at Portchester during the late Roman period little is known. Burials of children within the walls from about 300 onwards suggest that a mixed community then inhabited the site. It is possible that the population was entirely civilian and included soldiers only at times of crisis. Alternatively there may have been a permanent military presence either in the form of a garrison or of a community of *laeti*, paramilitary settlers drawn from other Roman provinces to secure the borders of the empire. There is very little evidence to indicate which is the most likely, and wider academic debates about the late Roman empire have been invoked to throw light on the problem. Crucial in these debates is a document called the *Notitia Dignitatum*, a list of civil and military posts in the Roman empire probably drawn up in the late fourth century. Among the officials it lists is the 'Count of the Saxon Shore', a commander of a series of forts along the south and east seaboards of England. Several of these forts can still be identified, but it is not clear if Portchester is among them. Nevertheless, some scholars have associated it with one of those listed, a certain *Portus Adurni*.

The forts of the Saxon Shore, as illustrated in a medieval copy of the Notitia Dignitatum

Such an identification, if correct, would suggest that Portchester had an active military role in the fourth century. The term 'Saxon Shore' might be applied to these forts either because they served as frontier defences against pirates of Saxon origin or because the *laeti* garrisoning them were Saxons. Whether or not Portchester is mentioned in the *Notitia Dignitatum* some pottery and other finds from the excavations do suggest that the population of the fort had some Saxon connection.

SAXON PORTCHESTER

It is unlikely that the fort at Portchester was ever entirely abandoned after the collapse of the Roman empire, but evidence for its occupation during the fifth century is slight. Pottery and other finds suggest the settlement of the site was continuous from approximately 500 through to the Norman Conquest of 1066. Owing to the very limited evidence available, it is difficult to say much about the physical appearance of Portchester in this period beyond the fact that the Roman defences probably remained little changed. The density of occupation within the fort enclosure evidently fluctuated, and the development of the interior with buildings was irregular. Some parts of the fort were ploughed and cultivated. Aside from the foundations of several huts the most important structure to have been excavated is a tenth-century residence with a hall and tower, possibly a belfry, in the south-west quarter of the fort. Bell towers were one mark of the house of a thegn – a man of knightly rank – so this may have been one such and a residence of some importance.

Documentary sources provide little further information about the site in this period. An entry in the *Anglo-Saxon Chronicle* for 501 records the death of a high-ranking man during a raid on the area of

PETER DUNN

A reconstruction drawing of the south-west corner of the fort in the late tenth century. The excavated remains of a stone tower and hall suggest that a thegn's house, depicted here, may have stood within the fort

A reconstruction drawing of the castle inner bailey about 1120. The defences of the bailey were probably first constructed in earth and timber

Portsmouth, and it is possible that Portchester was the place at which he was slain. But it is not until 904 that the first unequivocal mention of Portchester occurs. In that year Edward, King of the West Saxons, received *Porceastra* from the Bishop of Winchester. About this time the fort was turned into a burgh, one in a series of fortified bases intended to defend the kingdom of Wessex from Viking attack.

Norman Portchester

In the aftermath of the Norman Conquest of 1066 William the Conqueror (reigned 1066–87) granted Portchester to a powerful associate, William Maudit. Maudit probably founded the castle here, though when he did so is not clear. The Domesday Survey of 1086 makes no mention of a castle, only of a *halla*, or hall. But Domesday often fails to mention castles, and the defences of Portchester could already have been occupied. The form of Maudit's castle is also uncertain. He probably created the inner bailey, protecting its buildings with a ditch and timber palisade. He may also have built the eleventh-century inner arch of the Watergate as part of a new entrance to the fort enclosure.

When William Maudit died about 1100 his estates passed to his son Robert, another leading figure in Anglo-Norman politics. Robert was drowned along with Henry I's son in the White Ship disaster of 1120 and the castle – still undocumented – is believed to have passed a few years later, with the hand of Robert's daughter, to another powerful magnate, William Pont de l'Arche. He presumably held it until his death in 1148 and was probably responsible for redeveloping it in stone. Critical in dating and attributing his work in the absence of documentary evidence is the fabric of the present parish church of St Mary in the fort enclosure.

BRITISH LIBRARY, MS COTTON CLAUDIUS DII, FOL. 45V

The White Ship disaster touched many great families, including the Maudits. Here its effect on the descent of the English Crown is illustrated

About 1128 William founded an Augustinian priory within the walls of the Roman fort. The foundation charter implies that a church already existed on the site, though no trace of this has yet been discovered. The present building – which now serves as the parish church – was constructed for his new community in the 1130s. A new set of monastic buildings must also have been begun at this time, though nearly all trace of these has disappeared. Work on these buildings may never have been completed, however, because between 1147 and 1150 the community moved to a new site at nearby Southwick. The architectural details of the church compare with the inner bailey wall and its associated buildings, including the keep, which may consequently be attributed to William.

It is not clear who inherited the castle after the death of William Pont de l'Arche in 1148: either his son or a certain William Maudit, a descendant and namesake of the founder of the castle. Confusingly, the future Henry II (reigned 1154–89), while heir apparent to the throne, also granted the castle in 1153 to a certain Henry Maudit, the son of William. This grant is the first document to record the castle's existence, but it appears not to have been honoured by Henry II when he came to the throne the following year. Instead he took over the castle as a great royal stronghold, in which role it continued throughout the high Middle Ages.

THE ROYAL CASTLE

One consequence of royal ownership is that there is an increasing quantity of documentary information about Portchester from the 1160s onwards. Particularly valuable for the history of the early development of the castle are the so-called Pipe Rolls, the

The richly carved Romanesque font in the Augustinian priory church (now the parish church of St Mary)

accounts of the royal Exchequer. They record repairs in 1183 to a royal residence separate from the keep, which presumably stood in the inner bailey. The keep is also referred to in 1174, though the small sums then expended on it could not account for any major works to the building. It is generally supposed, therefore, that the twelfth-century heightening of the keep took place before the castle came into royal ownership.

For Henry II, as for successive English kings, the importance of Portchester depended in large part upon its situation commanding a harbour with easy access to the Continent. Visiting his vast territorial possessions stretching to the Pyrenees, Henry II regularly passed through Portchester, and it figured in his celebrated dispute with St Thomas Becket. Henry also used the castle as a prison for important captives such as the Earl of Leicester and his wife, and as a safe haven for shipping his treasury to France in 1163. During the rebellion of 1174 the castle was made ready to withstand an assault. It was armed with catapults, the wall walks were enclosed with wooden galleries called brattices and a garrison of ten (later twenty) knights was installed.

King John regularly stayed at Portchester to hunt in the neighbouring Forest of Bere

BRITISH LIBRARY, COTT CLAUD DII, FOL. 113

King John (reigned 1199–1216) visited the castle regularly during his reign and built a new chamber and 'wardrobe' here in 1211. With its neighbouring hunting park in the Forest of Bere it was an attractive site for royal recreation, and John is known to have brought his hunting dogs here in 1214. The bones of birds used in the lordly sport of falconry have also been found in the late twelfth-century levels of the excavations. But hunting was not the only royal pastime at Portchester. John also gambled here, as is known from a gaming loan of 10 shillings made to his brother the Earl of Salisbury during one visit in 1206.

John's memories of Portchester cannot have been entirely pleasant. It was probably here in 1204 that he heard the disastrous news of the fall of his own duchy of Normandy to Philip Augustus, King of France. And it was from Portchester in 1205 and 1213 that he twice prepared massive expeditions to recapture his lost inheritance. To his great frustration neither expedition ever left the shores of England. The king was also at Portchester on 26 March 1208, when the papal interdict caused the suspension of every religious ceremony in England.

In 1216 John's political misfortunes culminated with the invasion of England by Prince Louis, the son of Philip Augustus. Louis' invasion campaign was initially a triumphant success, and Portchester surrendered to him in June, after both London and Winchester had fallen. The castle was retaken in the spring of 1217 by John's successor, Henry III (reigned 1216–72). Without resources to man it, Portchester was one of several castles in the area ordered for destruction. But if the order was ever followed, the damage done cannot have been great, and the castle was restored the following year. It was then repeatedly used by Henry III as a point of embarkation and return for his campaigns in France.

Edward I (reigned 1272–1307) granted Portchester to his mother in 1273 and after 1299 to his wife. There is little documentation relating to the castle over this period, though the buildings were described as ruinous in a survey of 1274. In 1289 the castle mill was repaired, and in 1296 there is record of a wooden tower being constructed to strengthen the Roman wall along the sea front.

JOHN GOODALL

The early fourteenth-century inner bailey gatehouse vault. The chase for a lost portcullis to close the entrance is also visible

The castle was returned to the king in 1317 and there followed a period of intensive use and architectural development. Fearful of French invasion, Edward II (reigned 1307–27) garrisoned the castle and between 1320 and 1326 set its buildings in order at a cost of over £1,100, then a very substantial sum. As part of this work he extensively remodelled the buildings of the inner bailey and enclosed the keep forebuilding with new structures, now demolished. He also extended the main gate to the outer bailey and substantially reworked the Landgate and Watergate.

Curiously, within ten years the castle and its defences were apparently again in serious disrepair. A survey of 1335 describes many of its buildings as ruinous and reports that the sea had broken through the south wall of the Roman fort. Edward III (reigned 1327–77) immediately undertook repairs, building

TERRY BALL

A reconstruction drawing of the castle as it appeared about 1399. Note the newly completed Ashton's Tower and the structures enclosing the forebuilding

A depiction of the English victory over the French at Crécy in 1346

a defence by the Watergate to prevent galleys from sailing through the breaches in the Roman wall. At the same time an outer defence was created along the landward side of the fort. After 1356 the domestic buildings of the inner bailey were extensively repaired, and in the following decade the sea wall was properly repaired. The castle was also garrisoned and fully armed. But the defences of Portchester were never put to the test. Nor did Edward III often stay at the castle, though in 1346 he prepared here for the campaign that culminated in his great victory over the French at Crécy.

The last important medieval alterations at Portchester were undertaken by Richard II between 1396 and 1399. Shortly after arranging a peace treaty with the French, sealed by his marriage to the seven-year-old Isabelle of France, he began work to the existing royal apartments in the inner bailey. At the same time the keep was remodelled and the Landgate recast in its present form. A complete set of building accounts survives for these operations, which were supervised by the master mason Walter Walton. Work was pressed forward with great speed and sometimes the workmen were even

This altarpiece, the Wilton Diptych, was probably painted between 1395 and 1399. It shows a youthful Richard II being presented to the Virgin Mary by Saints Edmund, Edward and John the Baptist

issued with candles so that they could work after nightfall. By 1398 the shells of the new buildings were largely complete and began to be fitted out with woodwork and glass. But Richard probably never saw his new buildings because in 1399 he was deposed and murdered.

THE LATE MEDIEVAL AND TUDOR CASTLE

It is conventional to think of Portchester after the death of Richard II as passing into decline and obscurity, from which it was briefly reprieved by one notable event celebrated by William Shakespeare. In 1415, while Henry V (reigned 1413–22) prepared at Portchester for the campaign against the French at Agincourt, a plot to depose him was exposed. It was almost certainly within the castle walls that he confronted the conspirators – among them Richard, Earl of Cambridge, Henry, Lord Scrope, and Sir Thomas Grey. Having found them guilty of treason, he had them sent to Southampton and executed.

But although Portchester was increasingly overshadowed in both economic and military terms by the developing town of Portsmouth, it was far from forgotten. Despite a depressing survey of 1441 in which the castle is described as being 'right ruinous and feeble', Portchester was chosen as the landing place for Henry VI's French bride, Margaret of Anjou, in 1445, and in the 1490s its buildings were repaired. In 1501 minor repairs were undertaken to the keep, and in 1527 a military storehouse was built in the south-west section of the Roman fort enclosure. This building was demolished, probably in the 1580s, but its footings are still faintly visible in the grass, especially in summer.

In October 1535 Henry VIII (reigned 1509–47) and Anne Boleyn visited Portchester Castle, from where the king is reported to have gone out hawking every day. He subsequently ordered repairs to the castle, but it is not clear if any work was done. In 1563 it was used as a military

BRIDGEMAN ART LIBRARY/ BRITISH LIBRARY ARUNDEL MS 38, FOL. 37

Henry V as Prince of Wales receives The Regement of Princes *from its author, Thomas Hoccleve, c. 1412-13*

The foundations of the storehouse built in 1527 are still sometimes visible in the grass of the fort enclosure

ASHMOLEAN MUSEUM, OXFORD

The monument of Thomas Cornwallis survives in the church. He substantially remodelled the inner bailey before 1609

hospital for the sick and wounded from the French wars, and in 1583 its fortifications were put in readiness for a Spanish invasion. Elizabeth I (reigned 1558–1603) held court here in 1603, and shortly afterwards Sir Thomas Cornwallis, constable of the castle, completely remodelled the eastern ranges of the inner bailey. A survey of the castle made in 1609 by the royal surveyor John Norden describes the new buildings as 'containing four fair lodging chambers above and as many rooms for office below'. He also records that the work cost over £300 but implies that it was left unfinished.

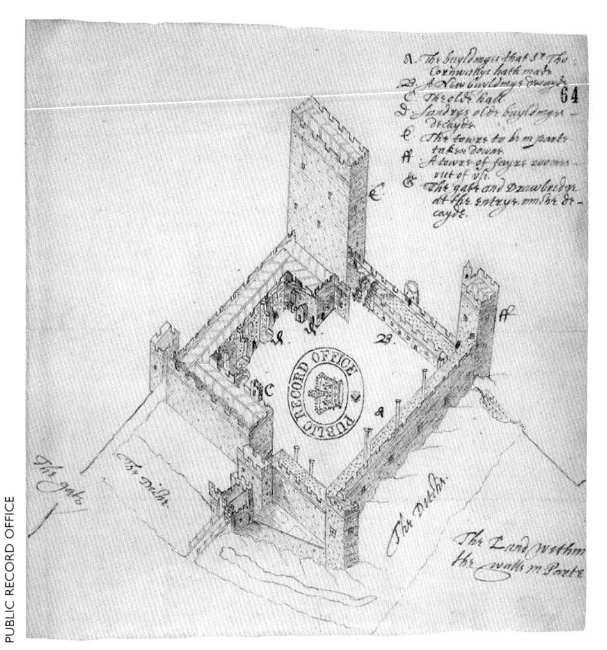

PUBLIC RECORD OFFICE

A sketch of the inner bailey made as part of John Norden's survey of the castle in 1609

The castle as a prison

In 1628 it was suggested that the castle should be developed as a naval storehouse, but four years later a local landowner, Sir William Uvedale, purchased it from Charles I (reigned 1625–49). Ownership of the castle has descended ever since through his heirs, the Thistlethwaite family. Sir William repaired the buildings in order to lease them out, and their subsequent history has been both varied and surprising. In 1644, during the Civil War, a detachment of Parliamentarian dragoons briefly quartered here, but the castle saw no action. Twenty years later, in 1665, it was used to house about 500 prisoners taken during the Second Dutch War. Some of them were lodged in the parish church and were responsible for burning it down; the damage was not properly repaired until 1706.

The castle was again pressed into service as a prison during all the major conflicts of the eighteenth century. Although it was first leased by the Crown for this purpose between 1702 and 1712, during the War of the Spanish Succession, the life of the prisoner-of-war camp is not documented in detail until Britain's various hostilities between 1740 and 1763. The prison quarters were originally restricted to the inner bailey with a guardhouse outside the gatehouse. Complaints were made by the prisoners in 1742 about the cramped conditions, and there were

PORTSMOUTH CITY MUSEUMS AND RECORD OFFICE

A view of the castle interior engraved in 1733, showing the prisoners milling around within a specially created exercise yard

riots the following year. In response the Admiralty gave permission for a fenced airing ground to be constructed in the fort enclosure, the Roman walls being too ruinous to form an effective barrier to escape.

Overcrowding continued to be a problem, however, with the number of prisoners rising from 1,100 in 1746 to about 2,500 late in 1747, almost a quarter of the prisoner-of-war population in England at the time. A system of exchanging prisoners with captured British servicemen meant that few remained in confinement for more than a year. The men slept on shared beds within a regulation space 0.75 m (2 ft 6 in) wide and 1.8 m (6 ft) long and were fed a carefully prescribed diet provided by private contractors. Captured officers received pay of a shilling per day and were given considerable liberties, being allowed to leave the castle with a guard. In 1760 one French prisoner married a local woman, and a child of theirs was later baptised in the parish church. Curiously, the prison guards themselves were poorly accommodated, with insufficient barrack space. In 1760 Edward Gibbon, then a budding scholar of Roman history, briefly

NATIONAL PORTRAIT GALLERY

A caricature of Edward Gibbon in his militia uniform

THE PRISONERS ❖ OF WAR ❖

Life within the prison during the Revolutionary and Napoleonic Wars with France appears to have been regulated in much the same way as in the 1760s. But, reflecting the scope of the war, the prisoners came from across the globe. Besides Europeans and Americans there were also West Indians, who had to be issued with extra clothes to protect them from the cold. Foreign nationals were commonly recruited to the ranks of the British army, a situation that could spark trouble in the prison. In 1810, for example, 120 German and Swiss prisoners volunteered for the Sicilian Regiment, and when they went to collect their uniforms a riot ensued, the French threatening to kill them. Women, children and other civilians innocently caught up in the war were also held here, though they were usually exchanged with British prisoners or released as quickly as possible.

There is much graffiti by prisoners in the castle. This inscription is in the inner bailey angle tower

took command of Portchester as an officer in the Hampshire Militia with '4 subalterns, 7 serjeants, 9 corporals and 214 privates to guard about 3,200 prisoners. The place was agreeable for the officers who boarded in neat private houses and lived very well, but it was very bad for the men. The prison was very loathsome and the men's barracks not much better'.

After the Treaty of Paris in 1763 Portchester was emptied of prisoners, and its medieval buildings, still under military control, were left to fall into ruin. But in 1794 work began again to fit it up for prisoners as Britain was stirred to war in the aftermath of the French Revolution. Thirteen new timber houses were erected in the fort enclosure to house 500 men each, and proposals were put forward to alter the keep and its adjacent buildings to hold 1,000 more men. The castle appears to have remained in largely this form for the remainder of its working life as a prisoner-of-war camp, which continued with an eight-year break between 1802 and 1810 (when it was used as an ordnance depot) until the defeat of Napoleon.

The prison was self-sufficient in most respects, as the varied skills of the prisoners themselves supplied its needs. Many of the prisoners also practised crafts such as bone-carving, creating such items as combs, dominoes and devotional objects.

PORTSMOUTH CITY MUSEUMS AND RECORD OFFICE

A view of the castle as a prison by a former prisoner, Louis Garneray, dated 1817. It illustrates the degree to which the interior of the fort was built up

The model ships made by them were particularly valued, and such was the quality of lace-making in the prison that it was forbidden as a threat to the local industry. Inmates could trade all these items along the main road of the fort, which was fenced off from the prison enclosure and accessible to the villagers. In 1811 some prisoners were caught forging money.

For entertainment a theatre troupe was organised, and its productions included *The Barber of Seville*, sung to the accompaniment of a twelve-piece orchestra. Performances were initially open to the public, but such attendance was later forbidden. This theatre was also popularly held responsible for a murder in 1813. According to the *Hampshire Telegraph*, one prisoner stabbed another 'on account of his superior talent in writing these little pieces for the stage'. The guilty party was tried and hanged before a great gathering of 7,000 fellow prisoners, who expressed '...astonishment at the novelty of the sight, it being the custom in their country either to shoot or guillotine criminals'.

The last prisoners of war left the castle by May 1814, after which it served briefly as a hospital and then as a prison for deserters. In 1819 it was finally abandoned by the army and returned to the Thistlethwaite family. They presumably demolished most of the remaining prison buildings. A proposal was made in 1855 to convert the castle into a military hospital, but a purpose-built one was

This inlaid wooden box contains a Crucifixion scene cut in bone. It is one of several surviving curiosities made by prisoners at Portchester

PORTSMOUTH CITY MUSEUMS AND RECORD OFFICE

PHOTOGRAPHS COURTESY MR W PRICE

Historic photographs of the castle and its surroundings

constructed instead at Netley, near Southampton. The castle stood as a ruin for more than half a century until, in 1926 the Thistlethwaites placed it in the guardianship of the Office of Works, which undertook a massive clearance operation. Many of the workers employed in the project were unemployed miners. In 1984 the castle passed into the possession of English Heritage, in whose hands it still remains.

Acknowledgements

The author would particularly like to thank Julian Munby, Robert Gowing, Jonathan Coad, Karen Lundgren, Kevin Booth, Richard Plant, Derek Renn, David Park, Sharon Cather, Jeremy Ashbee and Bruce and Dervla Finch for their help in producing this guide.

Further Reading

B. Cunliffe and others, *Excavations at Portchester Castle, Society of Antiquaries Research Reports Series,* in five volumes.

H. Colvin and others, *The History of the King's Works,* volumes 1-5.